WATASHI

Selected Shuntaro Tanikawa Volumes

Naked (Stonebridge/Saru, 1988)
Minimal (Shichosha, 2002)
A Chagall and a Tree Leaf (Katydid, 2008)
Two Billion Light-Years of Solitude (Shueisha, 2008)
62 Sonnets + 36 (Shueisha, 2009)

Translations by Shuntaro Tanikawa

Mother Goose Rhymes
Peanuts

Watashi

Shuntaro Tanikawa

Translated by William I. Elliott & Kazuo Kawamura

VAGABOND PRESS

Acknowledgments

I (Watashi)
was originally published in Japanese
by Shichosha in 2007.

ISBN 978 0 9805113 6 9

Vagabond Press, Sydney and Tokyo

© Shuntaro Tanikawa,
William I. Elliott and Kazuo Kawamura 2010

Contents

Self-Introduction **7**

A River **8**

Meeting Me **9**

A Scene **10**

It's Morning **11**

Good-Bye **12**

Keep Writing **13**

I Am I **14**

Deserted House (1) **15**

Deserted House (2) **16**

Deserted House (3) **17**

Falling Asleep **18**

2 × 10 **20**

Gazing at the Garden **21**

A Poet's Ghost **22**

A Defense of Poetry or, Why Novels Are Boring **23**

Epitaph for a Poet's Grave **25**

Mere Words **26**

Music **28**

"A River of Sound" **29**

Where Is *He*? **30**

Quotations from "A Quotation of a Dream" **31**

Eleven Variations on "Late Afternoon" **34**

Guided by Clouds **40**

The Sward of Life **41**

A Future Puppy **42**

Meeting Mother **43**

Into the Music **44**

I'm a Human **45**

A Rainbow Gate **46**

What Grandma Says **47**

You Who Are Crying **48**

She **49**

Music Once Again **50**

'Goodbye' Is a Temporary Word **51**

Immortality **52**

Immortality **52**

With a Rabbit **53**

Under a Tree **54**

Self-Introduction

I'm a short, baldheaded old man.
For over half-a-century
I've lived tossed about by words such as
nouns, verbs, postpositions, adjectives and question marks;
so I rather prefer silence.

I like tools;
and I very much like trees, as well as bushes,
but I'm not good at memorizing their names.
I'm not so interested in past dates
and I feel antipathy toward authority.

I'm squint-eyed, astigmatic and far-sighted.
I have no Buddhist altar or Shinto shelf-shrine in my house,
but I do have a huge mailbox that leads into my room.
I regard sleeping as a kind of pleasure
and though I have dreams I forget them when I waken.

What I'm describing here is factual
and yet I feel a false note is struck when things are put into words.
I have two children living separately and four grandchildren, and keep
    no dogs or cats.
I spend most of the summer in T-shirts.
The words I write are sometimes given prices.

A River

Sallow water was flowing hesitantly
and that was a river,
a descendant of shapeless things living underground.
I know the water is headed towards the sea,
but where it originated I do not know.

Just as the train crossed the river the young woman beside me yawned.
Something welled up from the dark depths of her throat
and I suddenly realized that my brain is dumber than my body.

Worrying that the physical part of me now being jostled by the train
is mostly made up of water,
the cerebral part of me is supporting myself with words.

Some time long ago, somewhere far away,
the volume of words was far less than it is now,
but the power with which they were linked to Hades was probably far
    greater.

Water, changing shape into sea, clouds, rain and ice,
remains on this planet.
Words, too, changing shape into speech, poetry, contracts and treaties,
cling to this planet.

So do I.

Meeting Me

Turning off the national highway onto a prefectural road
and then turning left onto a village road that dead-ends—
that is where I live—
the other I than I.

It's a shabby house.
A dog barks.
A few plants grow in the garden.
As usual I sit on the verandah.
They serve me roasted tea.
There is no word of welcome.

I was given birth by my mother;
I by a language.
Which would be the real I?
Though I've had enough of that sort of talk,
I suddenly began crying,
and choked on the roasted tea.

The shriveled breasts of my senile mother—
"That's the dead-end of my hometown",
I say, sobbing.
But as I look in silence at the daytime moon
I gradually come to understand that
both the beginning and the end are far more distant.

The day ended.
Listening to frogs croaking,
futons side by side, I fell asleep
and then both I and I became "shining particles of dust in the universe."

A Scene

A whirlwind standing on a deserted field,
having lost its way, is at a loss.
Exorbitant tears that evaporated and turned into cirri
now float in a corner of the blue sky on the verge of death.

Corpses litter the weeds
but no birds are seen pecking at them.
Signs of what was once called music
are drifting in the background like timid ghosts.

All the words up to now invented, spoken and written by people,
were from the very outset a mistake.
Only a silent smile,
directed at a new-born puppy, was just.

The lapping sea draws near the mountain
and one by one the stars close their eyes.
Is that because 'God' still exists
or is already dead?

The end of the world is calm and beautiful like this …

so I write just now.
In words I find nothing but my past
and see no future anywhere.

It's Morning

First I stretch in bed.
I sit up abruptly.
I piss.
I get the newspaper.
I am a tiny power plant.

The power of dead leaves falling …
The power of a fretful child's tears …
The power of the fading sound of a Jews's harp …
The power of casual punctuation …
The power of 'Good morning' …

An invisible matrix
binds microscopic powers.
I am one of those knots.
The earth is on the table.
I play a staring game with the earth.

I drink carrot juice.
I switch on the desktop computer.
I remain absentminded for a while.
Unexpected words emerge,
like this, like bubbles.

Good-Bye

Good-bye, my liver.
Good-bye, also, kidneys and pancreas.
I'm about to die now,
but since there's no one here
I pass all of you my farewell.

You've worked for me for a very long time.
Now, though, you're free.
You can go anywhere you like.
Having bid you all good-bye, I can also be utterly free.
I'm all soul—no make-up.

My heart, I've troubled you, making you pound and throb.
My brain, I've made you think of altogether senseless things.
My eyes, my ears, mouth, and penis, too, I've inflicted pain on you.
All of you—please! Don't hold it against me!
It's because of all of you that I have been myself.

Nevertheless the future without you is bright.
Since I have no more self-regret,
I will willingly forget myself,
dissolve into mud and vanish into the sky.
I'll become friends with wordless things.

Keep Writing

A train is running on a single track along the gorge.
Monkeys have already abandoned evolution.
The sounds of the wonderful old bagpipes have receded,
and I have nothing to do but keep writing poems.

A mother is on the sofa giving the breast to her baby,
and on a corner at midday there is suddenly an explosion.
On a new morning noisy opinions are heard
while a boy is sullenly reading a comic strip.

What does it matter?
The official history parades nothing but heroes
and only scratchy old photos remain;
while I have nothing to do but keep writing poems.

We can't find the ending
because we don't know the beginning.
Day after day we continue to doubt believing
and only the sky spreads out widely, like salvation.

Living with garbage that has nowhere to go,
forgetting missing people's names,
pawning what ought to be offered at the altar,
unable to tell a nanometer from a light-year,

being asked the pros and cons without time to breathe,
dodging back and forth between wavering feelings,
seeking a bliss deeper than meaning,
I have nothing to do but keep writing poems.

I Am I

I know who I am.
Though I'm here now,
I may soon be gone.
Even if gone, I'm still myself,
but in fact I don't have to be myself.

I'm partly grass.
I may be partly fish.
Though I don't know what it's called,
I'm also a dully shining ore.
And of course I'm almost you.

Because I cannot vanish even after being forgotten,
I'm a melody that will be repeated.
I'm a faint wave and particle
that has arrived from light-years hence,
riding, excuse me, on the beat of your heart.

I know who I am,
so I also know who you are.
Even if I don't know your name,
even if you don't have your name registered anywhere,
I'll go out of myself into you.

Enjoying getting wet with rain,
missing the starry sky,
laughing convulsively at corny jokes,
transcending the tautology 'I am I,'
I am I.

Deserted House (1)

A woman came into the house.
A man came in by another door.

Saying nothing, the man undressed.
The woman did the same.
She touched his belly with her right hand.

The street looked hazy through the dirty window.
The man plucked at her nipple.
A muffled voice …
The man entered the woman.

Their two bodies heaved on the dirty bed like the sea
and soon … calmed down.
Gunshot like popping beans can be heard in the distance.

Saying nothing, the man got dressed.
The woman did the same.

The man left the house.
The woman left by another door.

Deserted House (2)

If I remove one of the floorboards,
I may find a diary hidden there.
Refusing to be seen by people,
a host of letters and characters, which I hoped I could touch,
are quietly fading on the paper.
Their explicit expression has almost lost its meaning,
but their implications barely retain echoes of the delight of living.

"August 6, clear skies.
'God' speaks not in human language
but in a language of the sky, of wind and of crows,
of rocks, centipedes and poisonous mushrooms.
These languages we cannot hear unless we totally forget human language.
The first human mistake was to have named it 'God.'"

Violent plants have split the floorboards and are invading the whole room.
Ants crawl in a long line towards the tilting cupboard.
Some being once called 'God'
keeps on talking.

Deserted House (3)

A cloth easy chair covered in dust …
A toy man, "So-and-so", minus one arm, lying on the floor …
Someone took away the time before it had become a memory.

The wind faintly shakes the glass window.
Is it the heart or spirit or soul that is scared by the sound?
There are too many unnamable things here.

Two transparent figures are kissing.
A divided story and a national border …
From the distant sea the tide comes in slowly
and soon soaks innumerable documents.
A softly floating beach ball …
Invisible cobwebs strung about …

Those who once lived here—
where are they living now?
It might be ourselves.

Countless stroboscopes shining
before sinking like Atlantis to the sea floor …
Tomorrow brushing the tip of the nose …

Falling Asleep

A crow is cawing in the distance.
It's cawing fairly persistently.
What's going on at this time of night?
Somewhere a washing machine is whirring
and a nondescript sputtering is heard above the ceiling.

Outside the house a black space is expanding.
Though it should be filled with life
it brings to mind the English word 'void.'

[*The head hair and nails of a corpse keep on growing.*]

When did the world first take on this structure?
The midnight sounds I hear as I stay awake
become in my heart a music of the absurd.

*

Although I have nothing to say
I get up and lay out words on paper,
because I want words to lie about like stones.

In the face of violence a flood of meanings is powerless.
The same is true with tears
and, of course, with silence.

[*The head hair and nails of a fetus keep on growing.*]

But the silence hidden in words,
disguising itself sometimes as laughter,
sometimes as meaninglessness,
sometimes as song,
invites people towards the edge of this world.

*

A world resurrecting in memory of deep orgasm
exists in a different dimension from that of this reality,
like magma.

In such a crucible, between asleep and awake,
in a hodgepodge
of human races, religions, institutions, thought and illusion,
I await the first faint birth cry.

2 × 10

The morning mist of poetry is settling languidly
on the garbage of language dripping from this planet.

The cheek I touched with fingertips on that day
is now but a single line on a sheet of white paper.

The tongue is licking, without speaking,
what the eyes have failed to see.

All moments forgotten by the heart
are piling up on the soul (maybe).

Worn out walking on the path of words,
I squat on the labyrinth of silence and laugh.

A dictionary cannot measure the depth of a single word.
Vocabulary litters the shallows of intellect.

The language is a skin which adheres to reality's flesh.
Poetry is an endoscope which recoils from the darkness of the viscera.

What silence has left behind
after the overwhelming brilliance of tropes …

Meaning calls to meaning,
unable to bear the silence of twilight.

Night continuously advances
and in its depths tomorrow emits a faint fragrance.

Gazing at the Garden

I know
you have stopped reading poems.
There are tens of books you've read
still on your shelves
whose pages you no longer open;

instead, you look through narrow windows
at the garden overgrown with weeds
as though you'd like to say
you can read the invisible poems hidden there.
You gaze at the soil, ants, leaves and flowers.

"Sally has slipped off somewhere—where no one knows",
you murmur in a voice not quite a voice …
Is that your line
or someone's who once was your friend?
Even that doesn't matter to you now .

What has dripped from words,
what has overflowed words,
what has obstinately refused words,
what words have been unable to touch,
what words have killed …

unable either to mourn or celebrate these,
you are gazing at the garden.

A Poet's Ghost

I see a poet's ghost standing in a deserted house,
behind the windowpanes down which rain-drops are falling,
discontent with being just a name in a corner of a literary history,
discontent even with having driven a woman to death,
and too proud to be at ease in the afterlife.

No longer able to give voice,
he has turned into countless printed letters.
On the underground shelves of old and new libraries
he is still competing with close friends for fame,
finally unable to answer questions about poetry.

He believed he had read the heart of the blue sky.
He believed he had known why little birds twitter.
He had lived with people like pots and pans
and believed he'd understood the silence hidden in shouting and
    whispering,
shedding not a single drop of sweat or blood.

Beside the poet's ghost, the ghost of a rhinoceros
looks questioningly into its neighbor's face.
It doesn't know that the poet also was a mammal.
Everyone! Sing a lullaby indiscriminately
to all dead creatures, including poets.

A Defense of Poetry or, Why Novels Are Boring

"We [poets] are busy doing nothing." —Billy Collins

It's not I stomping footprints on a manuscript on the Notebook's
    white screen
which is like the morning of the first snow.
That's what novels do.
Thank God I can write nothing but poetry.

It seems that novels are seriously worried
over whether they should let a woman have a new generic bag
or a Gucci hand-me-down from her dead grandmother.
Hence begins an endless story
of suppression, love and hate.
Oh, God! Terrible!

Poetry sometimes forgets itself and floats in air.
That novels condemn such poetry as cold-blooded and naïve,
I can more or less understand.

Novels try to confine someone in a cage for over a hundred pages
and then let him dig a hole to escape through;
but the hole he successfully digs
leads to a narrow lane where he lived as a child.

And right there is poetry, nonchalantly standing by
a persimmon tree.
Sorry!

The task of novels is depicting karma.
Giving people unbridled joy—that is the task of poetry.

Novels take a winding path that leads to the ordinary world.
Poetry skips along a path straight to and beyond the horizon.
Neither of these can satisfy hungry children,
but at least poetry holds no grudge against the world.
Because it knows the happiness of wind
it isn't even afraid of losing words.

While novels irritatedly search for the soul's exit,
poetry sings with a drowsy voice making no distinction between the
    universe and old shoes,
and, riding on melodies orally transmitted by ancestral spirits, cheerfully
    warps
toward the day after tomorrow where human beings won't perish.

Epitaph for a Poet's Grave

"I who am infinite silence will give you words."
—Jules Superveille, "God Contemplates Humans"

When I was born,
I had no name
like a molecule of water.
But soon vowels were transferred to my lips,
consonants tickled my ears,
and I was called
and separated from the world.

Making the air tremble,
inscribed on clay tablets,
carved on bamboo.
recorded in sand,
words are onion skins.
However many are peeled away,
the world can never be uncovered.

I wished I could have become rustling trees,
having lost all words;
become clouds 100,000 years ago;
become a whale's song.
Now I return to anonymity,
eyes, ears and mouth stopped with mud,
fingers now entrusted to the stars.

Mere Words

for Chuya

Having turned into mere words,
the mountain is dimly squatting.
The port under an overcast sky
is thinking of something.

Is it like this in other countries?
The sea unconcernedly separates land from land.
Even the exclamation marks of the deep grief of criminals
have turned into mere words.

The merchant who stumbles but makes the best of it
is completely covered with electrons in the bathtub.
Even the love letters he wrote long ago
have turned into mere words.

A blue vein emerges
on a young woman's tied-up neck.
Poetry, having turned into mere words,
is about to peel off from the world.

That's not true! That's not true!
Why just mere words?
Didn't the page prick his thigh with his sword
to keep himself from dozing off?

—Quietness.
Now only quietness remains.
Scarecrows are down and out now
and meditate with straw brains.

Steaming rice
is served at some family table
in matching bowls,
faintly steaming.

Music

Gently nodding,
andante comes to an end.
The two chords are fleeting visitors.
They come from a distance beyond any meaning
and there return.

A spider is swinging in the wind
on the end of a thread as fine as a phantom.
As I watch it
finale begins,
anticipating the final silence.

Everything I have thought so far
is swallowed up in time's cave
and people go on living helplessly,
now pure as a murmuring brook,
loving the world.

"A River of Sound"

for Toru Takemitsu

A river of sound is flowing between trees and trees,
between thunderclouds and cornfields,
and probably between men and women.

You make its undercurrent audible to our internal ear
with piano, flute, voices—
sometimes with silence.

Music will never turn into a memory,
because it makes this present moment echo toward the future.
Nor will you ever cease to be.

Donning the clothes you've left behind here
I listen to the song you are singing over there,
as darkness slowly settles on the trees that surround the hall.

The verbal cosmos gradually recedes into the background
and in our ears we feel
the sigh of the world filled with contradictions.

Where Is *He*?

The summer when he was still visible,
the autumn when we could hear his voice,
the winter when I could pat him on the shoulder,
and the spring that didn't come again with him …

Yet he still repeatedly visits us,
bringing sounds to our ears
from beyond the silence.

The eardrums that faintly quiver
in touch with the sound waves from the invisible world—
another reality transcending meaning,
created by atoms of sound.

He is *there*,
listening with his healthy ears
to newborn sounds and to voices being revived.

Quotations from "A Quotation of a Dream"

Dripping water
… the silence of
concentric circles …

The sound is
in search of a place
to return to.

A shadow
silently
approaches,

waves agitating,
and the wind
throbbing.

The amorous words of beasts,
minerals'
sweet nothings,

and a flower
peeping into
an abyss …

Suddenly,
a clown
and a princess …

Time
places
punctuation.

Memory,
being tickled,
smiles,

and a castle
with a garden
and a dried-up fountain ...

Fragments of
bitter
conversations ...

Growth rings
answering
'whys' that arise ...

God's silence,
hidden in
scattering electrons,

recurs
like
a comet's tail.

Soul's
trees
rustling ...

Where are the people?
Coming from
so far away ...

Festivities
on the horizon
with Eternity as borrowed scenery ...

In the vacuum,
songs of
stars' embryos …

Eleven Variations on "Late Afternoon"

The westering sun
tinges the edges of the oak leaves,
merging into the lawn.

A swiveling window in the drawing room
mirrors the clouds
and timidly confronts the sinking sun.

Today has been another fine day.
The shadows of the westering sun
slowly lengthen.

*

The children have scattered
and gone home
in the westering sun.
An old man on the bench has closed his book
and has returned from the darkness of history;
but what reason has illuminated for him
are sinister weapons,
such as a guillotine.
The old man stands up, clinging to the faint memory of love
lurking in the haze of twilight,
and leaves the park for his nursing home.

*

A tree rises skyward,
recording itself in growth rings.

People, too, reach toward the sky
and wander out into the universe,

but their record has no center
such as that of growth rings.

In the westering sun
the twigs are golden arrows pointing to the heavens.

I wish I could cling to the tree,
believing

that the moment of its birth in the center of the rings
leads vertically to the universe.

     *

"You're transparent glass,"
the woman said.
"You can't retain light within yourself
because you're afraid of shade."

"You're a mirror,"
the man said.
"You reflect all the light.
Maybe you're also afraid of shade."

Backstage, the lighting technician is sweating trying hard
to create the light of the westering sun.

"We're using awkward words, aren't we?"
the woman said.
"Are we using the word 'light' as a metaphor for reason?"

"Then 'shade' might mean subconsciousness,"

the man said.
"Even light won't reach the viscera."

"Visible light won't,"
the woman said.
"But invisible light will persistently penetrate us."

    *

One afternoon deep down in the sea
the Dragon King's Palace is quiet and peaceful.
The Princess has long been dead.
Shellfish emit a pale blue light
and algae gently yield to the undulating tide.
Here time doesn't tick.
It only swirls, eddies and drifts.
Now and then a ship's sonar thumps,
but the mother-of-pearl palace door stays shut,
awaiting Armageddon.

    *

There's a firearm on a tea table.
A half-naked man is playing a cello beside it,
while yellow sunlight slants through the blinds.
The story at this stage is peaceful,
but soon a group of police surround this house
and the man while playing Bartok is shot to death.
… With such a story
the author herself (a 36-year-old woman) is getting bored.
The same yellow light as in the story is shining
on the white Mack truck the woman has driven until it's a junk heap.
A black cat is curled up on the couch.

From the distance comes the chimed melody of "The Evening Glow …"

It is heard neither in the story nor in this poem
but *now* and *here* in my ear, as I live and write this.

*

Drinking hot chai in a shop called "Afternoon Tea"
I was thinking
that meaning covers the human heart like mold.
Didn't words use to be more reticent?
They used to be just there, didn't they,
like a cracked tea cup, not overwhelmed by meaning?

A melody different from that of the background music now playing
is sounding faintly
in the depths of me.

*

Boys are fussing in the forest
because neither parents nor teachers would answer the morning
    questions.
They unconsciously decipher the shadows
lengthening in sunlight filtered through the tree leaves.
They must not rely on adults.
They must turn to the sea.

Neither legends nor fairy tales are trustworthy.
They leave the forest, walk along a stone path
and have already lost their way.
A small lizard in the grass is watching them.
A kite beneath the cirrus clouds is watching them.
No one helps up a child who has fallen.

The sea talks to them from afar
but they need to get older to know its meaning.

As the down on the cheeks glows increasingly golden,
the boys' pace grows slower
and finally they stop.
Where have the girls gone ?

*

She came late in the afternoon and said,
"I picked this up on the beach."
It was a piece of pale blue glass like a marble
washed round by waves.

"It's just ordinary," I said.
"But it's beautiful ... I feel it infinitely beautiful", she said,
looking near to tears.

She is no longer young.
Nor am I. Tonight is the wake
of our childhood friend.

Things that are nothing; things that don't matter at all;
things of which even the meaning of their existence is uncertain—
 "I feel drawn to such things" ...
I hear her say as I knot my black tie.

*

In your fancy, who am I? I wonder.
The face reflected in the rippling water—
Is that really my face?

Words extend their hesitant feelers between words
and glimmering images dissolve into darkness.
In your fancy, I count the afternoons that have passed so far.
Could that grief that was invaded by a golden light

also have been born from my mother's womb?

"There are questions that should not be answered in poetry",
you once said to me.
Who could I have been then
in your fancy?

    *

Ever drifting down the stream—
Lingering in the golden dream—
Life, what is it but a dream?
   (LEWIS CARROLL)

    *

There are things I've forgotten to write down. So it seems to me.
Probably something like cotton fluff? No.
Something like nebulae millions of light-years away?
There are things I've forgotten to write down.
In letters? In a diary? Or in poems?

Things I've forgotten to write down;
things I suddenly stopped at before writing them down—
where are they?
In the looking glass I see reflected a lawn of sixty years ago.
A young man is walking there.

Would I recall them if I talked to him?
If I went up and embraced him? If I stared into his eyes?
If I reviled him? If I hit him? If I stabbed him? Or,
is there nothing at all, anywhere, that I've forgotten to write down?
Even if I recall them?

Guided by Clouds

— Boy 1 —

Scattering the pollen of light,
the boy is waving his hand vigorously.
He can't help going in the direction
he was told not to go.

How does he choose
one among many-forked paths,
as with light steps he looks around,
guided by clouds that gradually change their shapes?

Because he doesn't know his true destination,
mountains, deep forests and murmuring streams
are like songs to him, until one day
the wounds he's got in his heart and body start to hurt.

With beasts, birds and insects as fellow travelers,
far from his mother and brother
and unaware that he has long been lost,
the boy has already merged into the scenery.

The Sward of Life

— Boy 2 —

Because music never ends,
I cannot stay here.
I go on walking across the sward of life
over the horizon of the planet.

Mom will leave here some day.
Dad, too, some day, with his cane,
will leave his temporary hometown,
leaving behind an empty glass marked with his fingerprints.

I think that's all right,
for everything is beautiful.
Nothing ever ends.
Wild flowers picked along the roadside are already just a fond memory.

As 'Goodbye!' turns into 'Hello!',
I'll come back from my long journey,
an unseen souvenir in my hand,
along with my younger sister who has never been born.

A Future Puppy

— *Boy 3* —

A future puppy that will love me
is wagging his tail on the verandah of a house on the cape.
I keep on writing in my diary
until the day comes when I'll see him—

one day about a forest chestnut tree,
one day about a cramp in my calf,
and one day about a beautiful orphan.
And so little by little I grow up.

Yesterday I went by myself to a planetarium
and saw the starry sky thirty-thousand years ago.
It was slowly revolving over my head.
Tears came to my eyes, I don't know why.

The day I'll be gone
the stars will still be shining
and maybe my future puppy
will be beside me.

Meeting Mother

— Boy 4 —

I went alone back to the old days.
Butterflies are fluttering under the cloudy skies of those old days.
A girl is watching them,
sitting all alone on the grass.

When and where did the feeling of loneliness originate?
As I sit beside the silent girl
I watch the butterflies mating.
She might possibly be my mother.

A road no one has ever walked along
vanishes into the horizon.
Only the faint sound of a string instrument
links me to this world.

The day when the distant future becomes the old days
I'll surely still be here,
having learned to love
and finding joy even in dying.

Into the Music

— *Boy 5* —

And then I walked through the music.
No people were there
but the square teemed with life
and there was a deep sea beneath it.

The lives of invisible trees passed by,
sins were trembling with the foreboding of being forgiven,
the memories of princes and slaves merged,
stars' eggs thickly filled the sky,

my body became transparent,
my feelings deep in my pink organs
had spread to the end of the universe
and dropped off the edge.

And I came back
with the help of the faint light of the amplifier's vacuum tube,
because I know that what dwells there
is also the proof of my existence.

I'm a Human

— Boy 6 —

I'm an aged boy
and an unborn old man.
The omniscient sun has been shining for us
for hundreds of billions of years.

I'm a human,
not an iguana, not a mushroom,
wishing sometimes to become a cirrus cloud,
sometimes aspiring to be a sperm whale.

My older sister left here last year,
leaving a short used lipstick behind.
I don't need to go anywhere
because everywhere in the world is right here.

Traversing the veins of fallen leaves,
I draw a map of life.
My dream will waken in the direction
in which my penis is sharply pointing.

A Rainbow Gate

— *Boy 7* —

A small suffering bamboo-leaf boat is floating
down the river of words spoken by everyone.
By the river of life I stand,
silently inhaling the scent of the water.

Because the heart can go everywhere,
however far,
I'm glad there are things I don't know,
even if by knowing our suffering would increase.

I wish a spring cold enough to cut one's fingers
would well up beside a dying soldier in the desert.
I wish a story that no one yet has told
would start there as if suddenly.

Did I love someone yesterday?
Who will I love tomorrow?
A rainbow rose like a gate to somewhere.
Someday I'd like to enter through that transient gate.

What Grandma Says

— Boy 8 —

"Everything is too much,"
says Grandma, sitting in the middle of the room,
though she has thrown away many things
as if they'd never been there.

Grandma's universe is filled almost to bursting
with countless stars,
with babies continuously being born
with people's words, spoken and written.

"Everything is too much, too much."
My father's mother repeats this like an invocation to Amida Buddha.
Because she doesn't think herself wealthy though she has too much,
she is now unable to tell any kind of story.

Grandma with her cute face and thinning eyebrows,
jostled by memories she can't easily wash away,
piles up in me
a cairn liable to tumble into the future.

You Who Are Crying

— Boy 9 —

Sitting beside you who are crying,
I think of the grasslands in your breast.
There where I've never been,
you're singing to the wide, wide sky.

I like you who are crying
as much as you laughing.
Sorrow is always everywhere
and some day will surely dissolve into joy.

I wouldn't ask why you're crying
even if it were because of me.
Somewhere now beyond my reaching
you are being embraced by the world.

One single drop of your tears is inhabited
by people of all ages, of all kinds,
to whom I shall say,
"I like you who are crying."

She

— Boy 10 —

I would have lived my whole life
just having loved her.
And having died
I would live on in her memory.

The blue sky that spread above her
belonged to me alone.
And the sun that brightened her cheeks
I would never give over to anyone.

In the village where she lives
beyond the snow-covered mountains,
she'll bear children
and will be surrounded by her grandchildren.

Happiness is transient like a vision
and remains forever underground like a fossil.
Now I can see
her serene pupils.

Music Once Again

— Boy 11 —

One day somewhere
someone played the piano.
From beyond time and space the sound caresses my ears,
even now making the air tremble.

A sweet whispering from far beyond—
I cannot interpret it.
I can only yield myself to it
like a tree that rustles in the wind.

When was the first sound born?
In the midst of the vacuous universe
like a code that someone secretly sent,
quietly and enigmatically …

No geniuses ever created music.
They merely closed their ears to meaning
and listened humbly to silence
which had been from time immemorial.

'Goodbye' Is a Temporary Word

— Boy 12 —

Having parted with the evening glow
I meet with night.
But the crimson clouds go nowhere
and just hide in darkness.

I don't say goodnight to the stars
for they always hide in daylight.
The baby I once was yet remains
in the center of my growth rings.

No one ever, I think, vanishes.
My dead grandfather grows like wings on my shoulders.
He takes me to places outside of time
along with seeds left by dead flowers.

'Good-bye' is a temporary word.
There is something that binds us together
far more deeply than remembrance and memory.
If you believe that, you needn't look for it.

Immortality

Immortality

You fly
over the sea of clouds,
wingless,
fearing the sky,
but serenely.

You fly,
not to escape,
nor to chase,
but because of love
held up by air.

You fly,
looking down over invisible houses,
tracing an invisible river,
imagining invisible mountains,
way up high.

You fly,
looking down on changing dynasties,
mushroom clouds beneath your eyes,
envied by gravity,
toward immortality.

With a Rabbit

He thinks of
putting the rabbit on the soft grass.
Gently, so it won't be frightened,
he places the rabbit
on the soft grass of spring.

The world won't yet end,
but as nothing is certain
at least he'll hold the rabbit
in his own hands,
and walk
up the hill
away from the aimless city.

There still remain things
not written in books.
Dwelling in that blank space
with the rabbit,

he hears a song,
which sounds like a prophecy getting outdated,
blended in with the wind.

Under a Tree

A child is sitting
alone,
knees together,
distant from everyone.
Time enwraps his shoulders like haze.

The moon is shining.
Sunlight is pouring down.
Stars are revolving.

No one can specify the place.
No one knows the way to that place.

A frog is looking up at the child.
An elephant is snuggling up to him.

Flowers are still in the bud.
The world is speaking in its stillness
the riddle in the child's heart.

A child is sitting
for us who are destined to age,
slightly smiling.

www.ingramcontent.com/pod-product-compliance
Lightning Source LLC
Chambersburg PA
CBHW030226170426

43194CB00007BA/877